CH

D0633270

DISCARD

Westminster Public Library
3705 W. 112th Ave.
Westminster, CO 80031
www.westminsterlibrary.org

MAY    2017

# 5 SECONDS OF SUMMER

## POPULAR BAND

Big Buddy Books

An Imprint of Abdo Publishing
abdopublishing.com

BIG
BUDDY POP BIOGRAPHIES

KATIE LAJINESS

**abdopublishing.com**

Published by Abdo Publishing, a division of ABDO, PO Box 398166, Minneapolis, Minnesota 55439.
Copyright © 2016 by Abdo Consulting Group, Inc. International copyrights reserved in all countries.
No part of this book may be reproduced in any form without written permission from the publisher.
Big Buddy Books™ is a trademark and logo of Abdo Publishing.

Printed in the United States of America, North Mankato, Minnesota.
102015
012016

**THIS BOOK CONTAINS RECYCLED MATERIALS**

Cover Photo: Jeff Kravitz/Getty Images.
Interior Photos: © 247PapsTV/Splash News/Corbis (p. 21); Associated Press (p. 15); Robb D. Cohen/
    Invision/AP (p. 29); KGC-243/STAR MAX/IPx/ AP Photo (p. 13); Newspix/Getty Images (p. 9);
    Chris Pizzello/Invision/AP (p. 31); John Shearer/Invision/AP (p. 19); Jordan Strauss/Invision/AP
    (p. 5); Charles Sykes/Invision/AP (pp. 10, 21); Brendon Thorne/Getty Images (p. 25); Michael
    Tran/Getty Images (p. 17); WENN Ltd./Alamy Stock photo (p. 11); David Wolff-Patrick/Getty
    Images (p. 27); © Debby Wong/Corbis (p. 23).

Coordinating Series Editor: Tamara L. Britton
Contributing Editor: Marcia Zappa
Graphic Design: Jenny Christensen

**Library of Congress Cataloging-in-Publication Data**

Names: Lajiness, Katie.
Title: 5 Seconds of Summer / Katie Lajiness.
Other titles: Five Seconds of Summer
Description: Minneapolis, MN : Abdo Publishing, [2016] | Series: Big buddy
    pop biographies | Includes index.
Identifiers: LCCN 2015034038 | ISBN 9781680780529
Subjects: LCSH: 5 Seconds of Summer (Musical group)--Juvenile literature. |
    Rock musicians--Australia--Biography--Juvenile literature. | LCGFT:
    Biographies.
Classification: LCC ML3930.A12 L35 2016 | DDC 782.42166092/2--dc23
LC record available at http://lccn.loc.gov/2015034038

# CONTENTS

# MUSIC STARS

5 Seconds of Summer is a popular music group from Australia. Its members are Luke Hemmings, Calum Hood, Michael Clifford, and Ashton Irwin. The band has been **interviewed** in many magazines. And, it has appeared on popular television shows.

# SNAPSHOT

**NAME** (*left to right*):
Ashton Fletcher Irwin
Calum Thomas Hood
Luke Robert Hemmings
Michael Gordon Clifford

**BIRTHDAY:**
July 7, 1994
January 25, 1996
July 16, 1996
November 20, 1995

**MAJOR APPEARANCES:**
*The Tonight Show Starring Jimmy Fallon, Good Morning America, TODAY*

**ALBUMS:**
*5 Seconds of Summer; Sounds Good Feels Good*

# STARTING OUT

In 2011, Michael, Calum, and Luke were high-school students near Sydney, Australia. They listened to bands such as Blink-182 and Green Day. The guys started a band and called themselves 5 Seconds of Summer.

**DID YOU KNOW?**

Sydney is the largest city in Australia. More than 4.4 million people live in or near the city.

# WHERE IN THE WORLD?

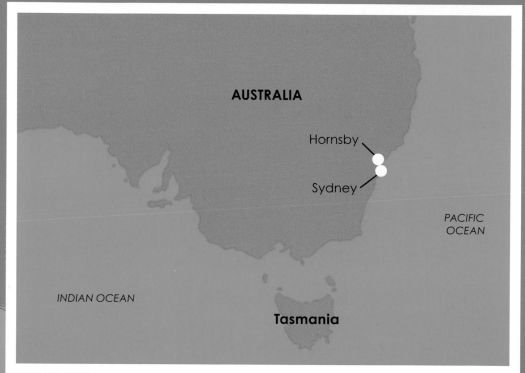

**AUSTRALIA**

Hornsby

Sydney

*PACIFIC OCEAN*

*INDIAN OCEAN*

**Tasmania**

5 Seconds of Summer played **cover songs**. The band posted its videos on the **social media** site YouTube. 5 Seconds of Summer quickly gained fans!

In late 2011, Ashton joined the band. Then, 5 Seconds of Summer played its first show in front of fans at the Annandale Hotel in Sydney.

Soon, major music labels noticed 5 Seconds of Summer. Sony Music offered the band a record deal.

Each member of 5 Seconds of Summer plays an instrument and sings. Both Michael and Luke play the guitar. Calum plays the bass. And, Ashton plays the drums.

# POPULAR MUSIC

In 2012, a famous boy band called One Direction posted a **social media** message about 5 Seconds of Summer. Then, One Direction asked the band to join them on tour! Soon, 5 Seconds of Summer had many fans!

One Direction is from the United Kingdom. It formed on a television show called *The X Factor*.

From 2013 to 2015, 5 Seconds of Summer opened for One Direction during world tours.

In February 2014, 5 Seconds of Summer's first big single came out. "She Looks So Perfect" quickly became popular in many countries including Australia and the United Kingdom.

The album *5 Seconds of Summer* came out in June 2014. The band helped write most of the album's songs. The album flew to number one on the Billboard 200 chart.

**DID YOU KNOW?**
In 2014, 5 Seconds of Summer's first album topped the charts in more than 12 countries!

Fans of 5 Seconds of Summer are called the 5SOS family, or 5SOSFAM!

# LUKE HEMMINGS

Luke Robert Hemmings was born in Sydney on July 16, 1996. His parents are Andrew and Liz Hemmings. Luke has two older brothers, Jack and Ben.

**DID YOU KNOW?**
"Please Don't Go" by Mike Posner was the first cover song Luke posted on YouTube.

Luke is 5 Seconds of Summer's lead singer. He is also the youngest member of the band.

# CALUM HOOD

Calum Thomas Hood was born in Sydney on January 25, 1996. Calum's parents are David and Joy Hood. He has an older sister who is also a singer. Her name is Mali-koa Hood.

**DID YOU KNOW ?**
In high school, Calum was a talented soccer player. He even traveled to Brazil to play!

In 2014, Calum and the band played at the MGM Grand Garden Arena in Las Vegas, Nevada.

# MICHAEL CLIFFORD

Michael Gordon Clifford was born in Sydney on November 20, 1995. His parents are Daryl and Karen Clifford. He does not have any brothers or sisters.

**DID YOU KNOW?**
When Michael has free time, he likes to play video games.

Michael is known for changing his hair color. His hair has been bright colors such as green, blue, and pink!

# ASHTON IRWIN

Ashton Fletcher Irwin was born in Hornsby on July 7, 1994. His parents split up when he was young. Ashton was raised by his mother, Anne Marie Irwin. He has a younger sister named Lauren and brother named Harry.

**DID YOU KNOW** ?

Ashton did not attend high school with the rest of the band.

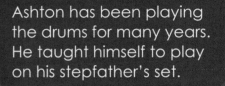

Ashton has been playing the drums for many years. He taught himself to play on his stepfather's set.

When Ashton is out in public, he is happy to take photos with the band's fans.

21

# TELEVISION APPEARANCES

5 Seconds of Summer reaches new fans when it appears on television. In 2014, it played on *The Tonight Show Starring Jimmy Fallon*. That same year, the band was **interviewed** on *Good Morning America*.

In 2014, 5 Seconds of Summer appeared on *TODAY* (*below*). Fans raced to see the band perform live (*left*)!

# AWARD WINNER

5 Seconds of Summer is an **award**-winning band. In 2014, it won New Artist of the Year at the American Music Awards. That same year, the band took home the Teen Choice Award for Choice Music: Breakout Group.

In 2015, 5 Seconds of Summer won Best Fan Army at the iHeartRadio Music Awards. The group with the highest number of fan votes wins this award.

In 2014, 5 Seconds of Summer won Song of the Year for "She Looks So Perfect" at the ARIA Awards in Sydney.

# STARTING A RECORD LABEL

5 Seconds of Summer wanted to have control over its music. And, the guys wanted to help other bands they liked. So, the group started Hi or Hey Records. The label's name was chosen by fans on Twitter, a **social media** site.

**DID YOU KNOW?**
A record label is part of a business that lets the public know about a band.

In 2015, 5 Seconds of Summer signed a pop-rock band called Hey Violet to Hi or Hey Records. The new band opened for 5 Seconds of Summer during their 2015 tour.

# BUZZ

5 Seconds of Summer continues to be a busy and popular band! In July 2015, the band put out a single from its second album, *Sounds Good Feels Good*. "She's Kinda Hot" reached number 22 on the Billboard Hot 100 chart. Fans are excited to see what 5SOS does next!

In 2015, 5 Seconds of Summer headlined a world tour! This means the band was the tour's main act.

# GLOSSARY

**award**  something that is given in recognition of good work or a good act.

**cover song**  a recording or performance of a song previously recorded by another performer.

**interview**  to ask someone a series of questions.

**social media**  a form of communication on the Internet where people can share information, messages, and videos. It may include blogs and online groups.

# WEBSITES

To learn more about Pop Biographies, visit **booklinks.abdopublishing.com**.
These links are routinely monitored and updated to provide
the most current information available.

# INDEX

Westminster Public Library
3705 W. 112th Ave.
Westminster, CO 80031
www.westminsterlibrary.org